I0115681

About My Books

The First Dozen

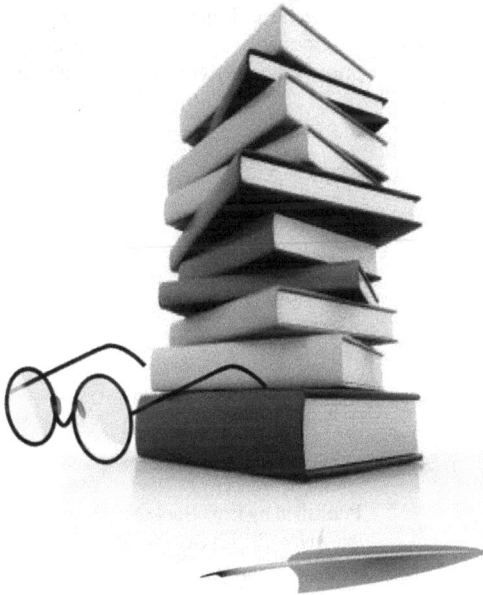

TOM OMIDI, Ph.D.

Copyright © 2016 by Tom Omidi

ISBN 978-0-9950982-2-0

All rights reserved. No part of this book may be reproduced, translated, or transmitted in any form or by any means—graphic, electronic or mechanical, including photocopying, recording, taping or information storage or retrieval systems—without the prior written permission of the publisher or the author.

Published by Eros Books,
Vancouver, British Columbia
Canada

contact@erosbooks.net

Printed in the United States

Author's Books
(As at 2016)

This booklet provides a glimpse of this author's first dozen books. After an overall description about these writings, a synopsis for each book is followed by one or more excerpts from the text.

[*] These four books have been re-edited extensively and reprinted in 2016 as well without introducing them as 2nd editions. All marketed books are now revised ones.

ONE

Theme

One theme—relationships—prevails in my writings due to its importance for personal and social health. All our lives, we are curious about human behaviour and confused about various relationships we have or wish to have. We often suffer in our relationships, or miss the absence of a reliable companion. In all, not merely the perplexity of this topic and my academic background, but also my sad personal experiences have goaded me to study and write about relationships. Strangely, exploring the softer side of our behaviour reveals even more darkness and cruelty about humans than all their blatant crimes. In fact, our attitudes and hypocrisy cause lasting tortures many folds harsher than all the killings that desperate and sick criminals engage in.

Despite the general theme, each book has its unique flavour and purpose. Fictions are intended to be mostly entertaining while addressing relationship issues too. Nonfictions are meant to be straightforward and practical for daily application and improving our lives. They intend to address the deteriorating social climate in modern societies, find the deep roots of the problems, and suggest long-terms solutions. Some of the earlier editions of these books have gone through a second intense review by the author and been refurbished in terms of writing style and rearrangement of topics, especially in the case of *the Nature of Love and Relationships*. Nonetheless, the objective for producing the second editions has been to make them easier reads for the public and to enliven the dialogues with more discussions and depth.

Although a tone of pessimism radiates in these books about the sad reality of relationships, society, and human nature, the ultimate message is one of optimism and desire for working harder toward a more harmonious humanity. We can be better human beings by revamping our egotistical mentalities and values to appreciate one another and life better. Therefore, the cynicism in these books must be viewed in a proper light. Overall, I remain quite hopeful, naïvely perhaps, to believe in the possibility of building better societies for ourselves.

TWO
Decades of
Contemplation

Two decades of contemplation stand behind these books. Findings from many case studies support the conclusions about the sad state of relationships and social chaos, yet only a small number of them are included as backgrounds. The latest scientific research also supports the conclusions unless more pressing findings by the author supersede and noted accordingly. Nevertheless, proofs for social sciences are always subject to speculation no matter how solid our arguments appear. While scientists strive to clarify our social and relationship issues the best they can, we need urgent solutions to defeat the rising social turmoil and improve our lives. Therefore, the books listed in this pamphlet focus on pinpointing social and relationship hurdles and finding practical solutions. Most importantly, however, the goal is to help us contemplate our life options realistically and adopt new mentalities for bringing more harmony into our lives. Everybody can associate with the daily social conundrums discussed in these books, including the philosophical thoughts, which are also for the ultimate goal of finding feasible options for living, peace of mind, and salvation. All we need as a first step is to agree that our present approach to relationships has failed and we need a new mentality.

I feel obliged to explain my unusual method of tackling several books together. For one thing, my routine of making notes about various ideas, before forgetting my intentions, often goes for days and months. Thus, projects are delayed, while I feel an urge to put my thoughts in proper contexts rather quickly. Another reason is that variety helps me keep a fresher mind when I re-edit each book later. In particular, writing a fiction alongside a non-fiction seems to boost both my creativity and energy. Meanwhile, I also worry about both my mental fatigue and the books' progress if I kept struggling with one book too long in search of acceptable results. Anyhow, my approach to writing is just one of my many quirks that have affected the workings of my brain and life.

Tom Omidi, Ph.D.
May 2016, Vancouver, Canada

THREE

Truthful
Fictions

My Lousy Life Stories
An abstract Novel

ISBN: 978-0-9783666-9-8   **Pages:** 354   **Words:** 113,200   © 2014

Instead of following a sequence of related events or a single plot, as is customary in contemporary novels, the intention of this book is to portray the protagonist's challenges and distress at various stages of his life through a series of intriguing and spirited stories. Yet, his observations and decisions during this long journey reveal the depth of psychological dilemmas and hurts that most humans must bear in the new era. In particular, the effects of our shoddy relationships alone ruin our spirits nowadays, while we also wonder about our choices and the purpose of our daily efforts and ambitions.

This is an abstract novel in the sense that fifteen independent essays and stories depict a commoner's unsettling fate and mind during his travels from city to city, while he staggers in the journey of life itself, satiates his curiosities, gets old, fights with his friends and family, encounters complex people and situations, and strives to make sense of it all.

Random Excerpts

I wandered around the city on the subway, baffled about my drifting identity in London—out of Tehran actually. According to the journey itinerary, I had to wait five days in London before taking the train to Southampton to board the U.S. Steamship. So, all I could do was to eat fish and chips every day, do some drab sightseeing with stress, and practise solitude. I spent one whole day at the zoo whispering curses about the hassles of being a human to animals and the pesky insects circling them. It was hard not to envy their simplicity and irresponsibility, though their blank stares felt purposeful and sardonic, as if mocking my stupidity. All day, I missed Haydeh badly, especially when the lioness glared at me and then yawned.

Maggie embraces the tree for testing and fails miserably. She wonders why she had even attempted to hug the tree when the outcome was so obvious just by looking at it. *Am I losing my mind or something, hugging a tree like an imbecile? I hope neighbours didn't see me!* Anyway, she tells Sheila about the engineer's comment and her foolish, failed experimentation. Sheila promises that she knows a member of the Council and might be able to influence or bribe him somehow to get the permit. So, at the end, Maggie just sits back, too, waits, curses Sheila, and wonders why Salvador is not asking any question or nagging about the tree anymore. He is not 'shooting' and 'shitting' around the house these days, which is so blissful and she thanks god for it.

Hearing someone on the portico, I lurch toward the foyer's narrow window and watch the mailman doing his tedious job. I can never do this kind of work... I admit I have become too fussy about jobs and organizations. Many of them would kill me faster than unemployment. So I am doomed one way or another. I have become a bum! Maybe that was why I lost my job in the first place? The mailman notices me, too, and nods timidly with a hint of pity, and perhaps some guilt for bringing all those rejection letters that only increase my depression and his workload.

Sherry was so kind to suggest that we take Rishard to a doctor immediately and get him some of those Vigora pills to mend his mood. But I said no. Because I was pissed off with both of them despite the idiotic grin on my face. She seemed concerned, all right. But more so for Rishard and herself. She was obviously unhappy about my visit ending sooner than planned. To me, however, she seemed too worried about Rishard at the time I was playing with the notion of getting rid of him altogether, even if it meant killing him—even if I ended up dead myself. (This story, *The Man in Charge*, is a classic if you read it carefully.)

Persian Moons
A Novel

ISBN:978-0-9950982-1-3 **Pages:** 468 **Words:** 141,800   2nd Edition© 2016

Darren Durant returns to Vancouver in 1988 after living in Tehran for three years and coping with the chaos of the Iran-Iraq war, including nightly missile attacks. He is now determined to establish himself as a painter and find a dependable companion. He had traveled to Iran after an agonizing separation from his beloved wife, Erica. Even the sacrifice to abandon his artistic life and work in Erica's flourishing software company as a computer technician had not saved their marriage.

A particular canvas he had painted in 1985 at the shores of the Caspian Sea keeps wreaking intricate emotional situations for him and others, especially a married Persian woman who follows him to Vancouver. Bizarre events obscure Darren's efforts to heal the scars of the war and his failures in marriage and artistic career.

Despite his intriguing romances, Darren grapples with the dilemma of committing to someone without getting emotionally hurt again, versus the prospect of ending up lonely and lunatic like his father. His lovers' competitions to monopolize him, along with plots by friends and foes for baffling reasons, further complicate his efforts to settle down.

Random Excerpts

Once off the gondola, he peers at his apartment on the opposite bank, as if to find his sneaky soul gauging him amidst the grand view from his regular spot on the balcony instead of following him. He both enjoys and abhors playing this silly game that is turning into a weird obsession. He has resisted the temptation of waving to his imaginary self teasing him from up there, except for once last month, when he could no longer de-

ny his ludicrous urge. He waved earnestly and watched by-
standers' reaction to his foolishness. Their tense curiosity—as
he had anticipated—to find the subject of his attention thrilled
him. Yet, he also worries that these odd impulses are perhaps
the early signs of his mental slump. *Did my dad's condition
escalate from similar silly urges and games? How much of his
crooked genes I've inherited?*

Darren struggled to curb his lust and fall asleep. However, a
huge urge to wake Erica to make love hampered his willpower.
Suddenly, his logic and legs out of control, he stood before the
guestroom and opened the door slowly. She lay peacefully under the blanket with the contour of her sexy body enticingly
vivid. His heart raced like a runaway locomotive, thrusting his
entire entity forward enigmatically. Unable to respire, unable to
reason, unable to resist anymore, and unable to regard his poor
ego, he plucked off the blanket and sprawled under it, embrac-
ing her slender body tightly and kissing her neck and cheek
tenderly. Her moaning in deep sleep pestered his conscience
shortly, yet he persevered, Erica unresisting, eventually joining
in, accommodating him, and relieving his mind to focus on the
job at hand. She enjoyed the make-up sex more than Darren
did, more than ever, but resisted showing it, out of spite, still.

Darren halts to catch his breath and pinpoint the image amidst
the spooky shadows covering the sidewalks and restricting his
eyesight. The man chasing him is concealed in the mass of real
and illusory figures, while the intense headlights of some cars
are starting to blur his vision too. A light rain is pasting his shirt
to his sweaty body. Hiding or running appears futile since the
source or direction of the danger is unknown. Still his legs appear to have a mind of their own, sprinting illogically. He gasps
a big breath and retries to discern his whereabouts and the path
to the apartment. He craves the opportunity of returning to the
house arrest status, instead of wandering aimlessly in the rain
and wondering about his destination.

Midnight Gate-opener

A Novel

ISBN: 978-0-9950982-0-6 **Pages:** 444 **Words:** 142,300 2nd Edition© 2016

This novel is about a young boy's perplexing journey through adolescence in a corrupt, fast-changing environment of Iran during the last years of the Shah's regime.

The playful, overly curious Kian Noori is anxious to solve several mysteries regarding his parents' history and lifestyle amidst the showy aristocratic society of Iran before the Islamic revolution. Then his life is turned upside down when a gypsy arrives at their home to tell his mother's fortune. He is not only mesmerized by her charm, but also perturbed by her peculiar predictions of his future and her warning about an ominous woman who would soon come into his life.

Special circumstances expose Kian to the adults' vulgar life-styles in lavish parties and nightclubs, so he loses his chance to experience youth like other teenagers. Instead, he is drawn fast into risky territories, including affairs with older women. All along, he is grappling with his cynicism about his friends, adults, and even God. Many other questions, especially the reasons behind his mother's malice toward him, also keep him on the edge. He eventually succeeds to escape his parents and the life of the bourgeoisie in Tehran in order to find peace in the new world. Still, his parents' extreme retaliations against each other lead to their ultimate demise when they get themselves entangled with the hectic justice system of the new Islamic government. Kian feels guilty for his inability to help them even as a learned psychiatrist practising in Los Angeles.

Random Excerpts

Narges gave me a rag and made me wipe the smoke's smudge off the walls. Then she helped Rahim bring a small table from another room and put it in the middle of the kitchen. She just walked around with only a towel wrapped around her breasts and upper thighs, like Tarzan training two dumb monkeys. She stretched her arms and legs to spread a new tablecloth over the table. She reached up to open the windows to let out the rest of the smoke and smell. I was afraid that the towel might fall any second if its knot loosened. She just made me madder every minute with her casual view of her appearance and carelessness about a possible catastrophe.

I was getting more addicted every day to the hoopla in Royal Club and other parties. Being a dance teacher for all those pretty women boosted my pride. Besides, the extreme symptoms of the bourgeoisie at the Club, including the gamblers' lifestyles and the vulgarities of the crowd on the dance floor, were turning into an invaluable educational setting for me. I felt I was learning a lot simply by observing the people around me. They provided lots of material for my diaries. Like a mad scientist, I filled so many pages with my new discoveries and feelings. These writings helped me fill my slack time when I was lonely and sad in one of my residences. Overall, the adults' attempts to win me over with their offerings were bearing fruits and I enjoyed their attention. I was adapting myself to their lifestyle, although I still resisted adopting their showy values.

My sudden fancy for the gypsy felt bizarre. She wasn't even as pretty as many gorgeous women around my family. Their glamour and heavy makeup had captivated me for years, especially at formal gatherings with their embroidered gowns and glittering jewellery, dancing long hours into the night to the Western tunes of tango, samba, mambo, waltz, and cha-cha. I enjoyed those plain miracles of nature when I wasn't too depressed. But this gypsy's effect on me felt special and magical.

Narges realized the game Father was playing. She swallowed her pride and decided to stick it out a little while longer. She appeared to be waiting for another opportunity to retaliate even harsher herself. Leaving him would be a foolish reaction on her part and an easy way out for Father, as if handing him his freedom on a golden platter. The way she looked spitefully at him showed how determined she was to make him pay real bad for everything he had done in Europe. I knew she would succeed. She would be able to come up with another brutal retaliation of her own soon. It was only a matter of when and in what form. Thinking about their upcoming games and retaliations against each other frightened the hell out of me.

Her white long fingers were so gorgeous, as were her feet, toes, eyes, lips, and hair. The red nail polish made her fingers and toes look even sexier. I enjoyed them as we just sat there, drank whisky, smoked cigarettes, ate chips and nuts, and chatted for one hour. We analysed the scenes in the movies we had been seeing together. As we got drunk, we talked more about the meaning of love and about many romantic tales in books and movies. Love was a new experience for both of us. Yet we felt like two experts on the matter. She, in particular, sounded like a love guru. She was thrilled for being in love at last, as if she had discovered it in me after a long painful search. Her romantic expressions sounded odd, though, as if she had forgotten our disastrous sexual episodes a few days earlier. Was she changing her position again about the importance of sex?

I could not believe my own eyes, holding Narges's hands with compassion. Maybe I was learning to be a real, caring doctor, after all. In the past, even thinking about touching or hugging her would have revolted me. Such a domineering lady now looked so helpless and resigned. She looked innocent, although some hints of her malice toward me and Father still rolled in my head. I caressed her hands with passion, delighted with my sudden enlightenment, a divine sensation probably caused by my sincere intention to forgive her. Uncle Mustafa looked pleased with my surprising adjustment too. Daphne would have been so glad about my maturing and learning to express affection. I was proud of myself too.

FOUR

Comprehensive
Nonfictions

Doubts and Decisions for Living
Volume I
The Foundation of Human Thoughts

ISBN: 978-0-9783666-6-7   **Pages:** 328   **Words:** 101,400   © 2014

Soon we should agree that humans' natural qualities do not match their common (idealistic) perception of themselves, and that this mental incongruity accounts for most of our personal and interpersonal problems. In addition, the characteristics of the environments we have gradually built around ourselves make it impossible for us to converge with either our natural or idealistic view of a human. Nevertheless, it seems as if we must face the same old cliché, 'Who are we?' even more seriously now, in order to detect the origin of our personal and social problems. Our findings would then make us wonder with even more surprise, 'Why have we become this way?'

Under the present circumstances, every generation learns less about life. Instead, the competition in society to give children all the privileges they supposedly deserve and more is too stiff to allow any one parent teach the reality of life and its hardships to his/her children. We get blamed for both not letting them live freely and warning them about their phony ideals. How can we tell our kids that all their dreams nowadays, including fame, love, trust, sincerity, and all the rest of those fantasies are only sure ways of losing more chunks of their independence, identity, and integrity?

Random Excerpts

Enough clues and warning signals are often around us about our misunderstanding of life, but we insist on ignoring them. Our frustration and anxiety often reflect our inattention or misinterpretation of the causes of our suffering. We feel helpless, as our struggles do not even bring us relief, let alone happiness. Instead, we feel desolate and lonely, and we get more exhausted and stressed out every day with our search for love and happiness. We try to correct the whole world and to make everybody understand our concerns. We like to inform our friends and family about our failing relationships and our needs. However, it seems, the more we try, the less we succeed to communicate with the rest of the world. Our frustrations and anxieties keep rising and we look in the wrong places for remedies.

Social and personal shortfalls are not new developments, but the downfall acceleration is now making us dizzy. Yet we are expected to adapt ourselves to this hectic condition more eagerly in order to survive. We feel obliged to set our life objectives according to some frivolous criteria of success and individualism. We must stay positive and pretend to love the life structure formulated around the interests of conglomerates and capitalism. So, we are burdened with a vast amount of unsettling problems and dilemmas, while our inner conflicts and doubts about our life choices keep piling up.

Nowadays, everybody, especially youth, feels defeated and doubtful about his/her purpose of living or even a simple, truthful definition of life. Yet, we must decide about many critical and urgent matters every day without reliable criteria and guidelines. Thus, we just make our half-hearted decisions and continue to live with our doubts, and life goes on. We only scorn ourselves for our inability to adapt to norms and rules that we have taken as life's reality. Unfortunately, all these sad clues and sufferings, evident in all aspects of our lives, do not teach us anything either. We do not stop and ask, 'Is the reality of life supposed to be so gloom?'

We can readily grasp and relate to the common sources of our sufferings. However, some deep causes of sufferings are due to the deprivation of our inner needs, including spirituality. This happens when we neglect to place sufficient emphasis on significant matters of life and to relinquish the majority of nonsensical desires, ambitions, plans, thoughts, actions, and decisions that we have been emphasizing on uselessly.

Doubts and Decisions for Living
Volume II
The Sanctity of Human Spirit

ISBN: 978-0-9783666-7-4   **Pages:** 344   **Words:** 102,000   © 2014

Understanding the realm of our spirit and learning how to empower it through a personally defined spirituality is the only way to survive life's hardships and perhaps find a relatively peaceful life too. As another natural wonder of the universe, fortunately, our urge for spirituality is deep within us like a conduit for appeasing our spirits. Of course, attaining this private sense of divinity is a personal challenge, which neither religions nor scholars can explain to us or help us with. We must set out to grasp it on our own in a hard way. Then, we can draw on this natural source of inner power and intuition to establish our personal beliefs, build our identity, and keep our spirit intact. Otherwise, we would just stagger along with the cocky crowd without knowing who we are and what the purpose of our living is.

An inherent link exists between our spirit and psyche, but it must be reinforced through self-awareness and developing a personal sense of spirituality. It begins with exploring our urges, psyche, and needs, which we must tune collectively in order to revamp our deluded mentality about life and being. Through a soul-searching process, we must somehow come to terms with our neglected and pained spirit and feel our link to the universe. At the same time, our invigorated spirituality bolsters both our psyche and spirit to redefine and enrich our lives, as explained in this volume.

Random Excerpts

Knowing (about) ourselves is a sacred crusade to grasp our existence and its potential value. The objective is to access our essence as a bewildered human and to understand the motives behind our thoughts and deeds within the finer realms of the universe (and not society per se). Thus, a definition of 'self' has evolved, mostly as a symbol of our idealism and the perfection we seek in ourselves. We hope to find a sign of humility and contentment beneath the contaminated and convoluted minds pervading the society. Yet, our search for 'self' also shows our despair and lack of confidence in the purity of 'who we are.'

Humans' unrelenting urge for spirituality is ingrained in their deepest unconscious as a primary personal need. In fact, this need manifests so instinctually we cannot help arriving at some fundamental conclusions. For one thing, our intrinsic drive for spirituality provides a plausible clue about the existence of spirit as a distinct feature of humans aside from their body and mind. Human spirit seems real and it evolves faster when we stir our divine potentiality to understand 'who we are.' In fact, while human urge for spirituality is responsible for finding and strengthening our spirit, the spirit within us is the force that drives our desire for spirituality.

The main struggle we endure permanently, knowingly or unconsciously, is our inner quarrel to attain a psychological equilibrium. Mainly, we strive to distinguish between the realities of this world, as we have learned or conditioned ourselves to believe in (the perceived realities), and the truth that is waiting to emerge from inside every intelligent human (the real realities). The struggle is to grasp and live with the contradictions between 'what we have become' and 'what we could be' in its purest form when God created us, free from societal influence. Generally, we try not to think about these contradictions. We rationalize who we are and what we do in order to reduce our pains. We deny our inner quest for the truth or its value. As intelligent beings, we know that wars, hunger, crime, genocide, destruction of environment, racism, drugs, and all the other manmade evils of this world are not the signs of a healthy life and mind, but we all propagate these symbols of civilization and conformity anyway directly or indirectly.

Doubts and Decisions for Living
Volume III
The Structure of Human Life

ISBN: 978-0-9783666-8-1   **Pages:** 326   **Words:** 99,000   © 2014

Life has become a stressful process and all the clues show that it would only get worse in the coming years, yet we must somehow manage our lives within this chaotic environment. Despite our eagerness to be philosophical about life and build ideal convictions, finding *practical* means of living remains a big challenge and priority. Living is a sacred, yet often scary, mission for us. All along, we must make important decisions and choose a life path based on some form of logic, self-awareness, and facts. We must grasp our real needs, set our life priorities properly, and move forward.

Our mission is to somehow fit within society, because most of us do no have the guts to live independently and think freely. Yet, we should at least know the price we must pay for the life path we choose. We should also always remember that we had an option to live differently. While the price for an independent lifestyle is frequent isolation and loneliness, mainstream life has the high price of hard work, humiliation, repeated failures, disappointments, and stress.

Random Excerpts

Most of our learning is *unconscious* through many *involuntary* processes. Our random motives to learn are usually superficial and transient, too, although they could lead to equally deep, irreversible conditioning traits and nasty habits. Conversely, real learning comes through a *conscious* process of awareness and intention to learn. It needs a specific objective, curiosity, and commitment, for enhancing the quality of our lives, e.g., by exploring our life philosophy. Conscious learning is also for subduing the alluring influence of our ongoing subconscious learning, which is too deep, severe, and 'self'-destructive.

There is a big difference between 'having to work' and 'wanting to work' for an organization. This is the distinction between the options of coping with organization work and being absorbed in it. Knowing our options and choices, as limited they may be, we can build our organization life rather effectively with deep awareness, high patience, and low expectations.

Most of us take our marriages for granted subsequent to a short period of honeymoon, after our passion settles and we touch reality again. This does not necessarily mean that we lose our love or enthusiasm that fast. On the contrary, we feel secure and comfortable in our marriage environment. This gives us the psychological safety and a platform to ensue our life aspirations more actively. However, relationship problems arise because we feel psychologically safe about our love and belonging needs. This is often not true. In fact, we have a wrong perception of marriage at the outset, as we assume that a normal (average) marital relationship would be problem free, despite all the stories and statistics that suggest otherwise. We assume marital problems emerge from those exceptional circumstances where partners are not normal or cannot handle their marital affairs logically. Thus, we see no reason to worry, since we consider both ourselves and our marital conditions normal.

To relieve our distress and agonies, we look outward to blame something or somebody. If partners trust and respect each other and have good communication skills, they can exchange compassion and sympathy, share their problems, and rid themselves of life tensions and stress. However, without trust and respect, partners feel spiteful toward each other. Their ideas and suggestions usually erupt in hostile tones and their marriage turns into the battleground for firing blames and nagging at each other. Having a marriage partner appears to be the most convenient way to relieve our tensions. And we like to feel, express, and receive love at the same time! However, the outcome is devastating over time when partners get carried away with all these needs unconsciously.

The Nature of Love and Relationships

Generally Acceptable Relationship Principles for the New Era

ISBN: 978-0-9938006-4-1 **Pages:** 542 **Words:** 150,800 2nd Edition© 2016

Over the last few decades, we have developed wrong perceptions about the nature of love and the purpose of relationships. With drastic changes in social values and lifestyles, our expectations from relationships have skyrocketed in line with our escalating personal aspirations. However, all these idealistic needs have only led to more distress for everybody.

The rising divorce rate and endless family conflicts reflect the hectic environment of relationships. These facts also reveal that our present methods of dealing with relationship hurdles have failed. While focusing on the symptoms of relationship failures, we have ignored the roots of the problems as a social pandemic. Thus, it is time now to recognize the complexity of relationships in new societies and analyze the real sources of family conflicts. It appears that we need radical solutions compatible with our new social values and expanding personal needs.

A main goal of this book is to help couples review their mentalities about the capacity and purpose of relationships. Another objective is to suggest a framework that can assist couples assess their relationships more realistically. It is time to appreciate the *need* for viewing relationships in a new light consistent with the characteristics of new lifestyles. Instead of searching all our lives for a soul mate and an ideal relationship, we must find a way to relate more effectively, while strengthening our identity and individualism too.

Random Excerpts

The inherent nature of love, particularly the effect of human hormones, shows that love does not survive in relationships in the form we usually imagine and desire. What we call love nowadays is often only a combination of lust, possessiveness, and insecurities we have compiled through social interactions and imitations. Accordingly, love cannot be a main success factor for relationships either. Only couples' ability to relate as well as their capacity for compassion, comradeship, integrity, teamwork, and knowledge of the relationships' specific needs can stir sincere passion and prolong their relationships. With people's increasing need for independence and self-reliance, couples would gradually adjust their mentalities about the limited role of love in relationships. Then they can enjoy both love and relationships realistically without assuming that they are necessarily the same or the cause and effect of each other.

A reason for conflicts in relationships is that couples keep arguing about the roles they would like to play, either jointly or independently. Each partner likes to set the rules for their relationship. This decision is often based on his/her rotating and abrupt preference to push his/her *need for independence*, (e.g., making investment or some family decisions alone), or *need for dependence*, (e.g., seeking support and attention). Thus, we need a relationship framework to eliminate conflicts caused by partners' erratic role changes, equality arguments, and arbitrary decision processes. Obviously, synergy is achieved better, usually, when partners work together to fulfil certain tasks or share decision-making needs of a relationship. However, synergy can be achieved also if couples support each other to perform their roles separately with real independence.

Even two compatible partners with reasonable expectations still find themselves in conflict regularly. This is because they judge the health of their relationship too emotionally, still based on their unfulfilled personal desires and demands. Their deprived needs lead to gross misperceptions about the health of their relationship and their partner's intentions. And then these misperceptions (mistrusts) further complicate their means of communicating and relating to one another. This is a most likely scenario even for two compatible partners with moderate expectations from their relationship. Now just imagine the level of conflicts and stress when partners' expectations have been set too high unrealistically at the outset due to their initial eagerness, Ego, optimism, or silly promises.

Obviously, our tainted social norms are responsible for relationship failures, which in turn damage society altogether. The only way out of this vicious cycle is to review our vision of relationships and reset it gradually to avoid further social downfall. Our *personal mentality* has to change in order to fit our newer social structure. These required changes are explained in this book. The *social mentality* about relationships and the government's role must be modified, too, in order to handle the complex nature of new relationships. We need less government interference in relationships, but a more progressive legal system in line with people's modern approach to relationships. Only with these personal and social changes, we might possibly reverse the fast declining fate of relationships.

Of course, it is hard to find the right social mechanisms when citizens' needs remain cluttered even for themselves. Couples do not know how to go about figuring out their true needs in a society overwhelmed by the ideas of consumerism and phony means of happiness. Therefore, they only get greedier and more demanding. Many superficial needs have tainted relationships and couples are not scientists to sort them out. They just feel those needs because everybody else around them feels the same needs and pushes the same values in their relationships. Meanwhile, the government is already too busy with so many urgent socioeconomic matters to worry about the real causes of relationship failures. Therefore, it just deals with the symptoms of this social chaos the best it can at a high cost to taxpayers. Governments are just waiting idly by for the course of history to define the relationship needs eventually. Accordingly, we can expect only more chaos in relationships, because neither governments nor couples are proactive enough in appreciating and overcoming relationships' inherent problems nowadays.

FIVE

Love &
Relationships
Series

Relationships Facts, Trends, and Choices
L&R Series # 1
The Bottom Line

ISBN: 978-0-9938006-5-8   **Pages:** 198   **Words:** 49,300   © 2016

Over 900 facts, trends, and choices about relationships in this book demonstrate the difficulty of satisfying this simple human need in the new era. They show the main sources of relationship conflicts and the consequent, rising personal frustration and depression. With our bizarre perceptions and values about relationships, we have indeed gotten ourselves trapped in an agonizing web of complex dilemmas.

As societies get more complex every day, our lifestyles and convictions have changed drastically. Accordingly, our relationships have become too difficult to understand and manage. Our personal needs, insecurities, and idiosyncrasies have also been increasing rapidly in line with changes in social values. However, we not only ignore the hazards of these rising personal shortfalls, but also justify our new needs and defects so obsessively and arrogantly.

An Excerpt

In recent decades, our relationships have shaped too closely around social environment and values, which merely propagate superficiality and arrogance. Therefore, the form and characteristics of relationships nowadays are not in line with humans' natural needs and capacities. Instead, we have created a social structure and relationship mishmash that is incapable of serving either humans or a civilized society. Especially, with women's new role in society and the decline of religious influence, we have developed many idiotic roles and demands in relationships. Thus, for assessing the prospect of relationships, we must examine the social trends, their impacts on relationships, and then find radical mechanisms that best correspond with the new needs of individuals.

Mysteries of Life, Love, and Happiness
L&R Series # 2
Eternal Loneliness

ISBN: 978-0-9938006-6-5   **Pages:** 214   **Words:** 63,800   © 2016

Unfortunately, we refuse to grasp life's sad realities and grow a more practical mentality accordingly. Despite our recurring disappointments and sufferings, we do not realize the pressure we are putting on one another with our naive views about life, mostly about an elusive happiness. We do not feel or admit that only by helping one another less selfishly, we might bear life's hardships together a bit easier. No one can elude, or do anything about, life's severe limitations in our wicked society, but only grasp and accept them with grace. Hence, it seems too idiotic and pathetic when we blame others, e.g., our spouses, for our stress and life's limited capacity to offer happiness to anybody. We are too naïve and stubborn to admit even these basic principles of social coexistence, yet try to discover the elaborate mysteries of life, love, and happiness. That is why our social structure and values are all falling apart too.

An Excerpt

Our confusion about the meaning of love and our 'desperation for a mate' would keep rising every year, because we cannot find or keep a partner or trust him/her in the long run. Obviously, this critical state is the outcome of drastic social changes and our rising idealism. We do not see the futility of our search for love or a soul mate. As more relationships fail every year, we get more desperate, which, ironically, only heightens our craving for both passion and compassion even more. In all, our obsession for love nowadays is a reflection of our rising loneliness and desperation for a companion, while our naive expectations (including love) ruin our relationships and we become even more desperate and lonely. This vicious cycle is destroying people's trust in each other and their expressions of love.

Marriage and Divorce Hardships
L&R Series # 3
Inevitable Traps

ISBN: 978-0-9938006-7-2   **Pages:** 206   **Words:** 59,300   © 2016

The effects of relationship hardships on people and society are rather obvious. The repercussions of our naïve mentality about relationships are overwhelming us too. Thus, our oblivion to see the cause of all these pains feels quite baffling. Our reluctance to acknowledge the depth of relationship dilemmas we have imposed upon ourselves, as well as their personal and social ramifications, is rather shocking. In fact, our ignorance, indifference, or denial shows the depth of our social numbness.

This book's goal is to address our responsibility in causing the rising personal and social instability, suggest some solutions to revamp our viewpoints, and seek better means of relating in our marriages—or at least evade this potential source of suffering by learning to live more independently. Instead of only bragging about independence, time has come to become self-reliant truly, which ironically teaches us the art of relating and depending on one another in a realistic manner as well.

An Excerpt

Partners' imperfections, which often appear normal individually, clash in relationships severely, and thus the degree of their incompatibility and malice increases many folds very quickly. At the same time, partners are unable to set their tolerance level realistically, because they have no reliable view of the expected (acceptable) level of conflicts in relationships. Without enough self-control and wisdom, they let their Egos drive all their decisions, including the matter of a desired tolerance level for a typical marital relationship. In fact, many people are less willing or able nowadays to live with the inconveniences of marital life, mainly due to their drive for individuality and a misguided sense of self-importance.

Gender Qualities, Quirks, and Quarrels
L&R Series # 4
The War of Sexes

ISBN: 978-0-9938006-8-9   **Pages:** 200   **Words:** 49,200   © 2016

Gender's physical and hormonal differences are obvious, but their behavioural and emotional differences have been a matter of interest, excitement, and irritation regularly, especially in the new era. Even more amazing, the more we have tried to learn about, and practise, gender equality, the more gender parities have manifested and the more conflicts have risen between genders. Overall, as relationship conundrums rise in society, we feel both obliged and intrigued to study gender mentalities and answer many questions in hopes of improving the health of relationships and society. For facing all these new challenges, it is necessary to view gender differences in a more productive perspective, instead of being cynical and critical too much about them. We must view them as a potent inner force that could help genders complement each other and increase efficiency in their relationships

An Excerpt

New social trends set the foundation for gender encounters and quarrels. We are living in a new era satiated with many shallow needs and ideologies by people who are too obsessed with finding love and happiness, but have no patience and compassion themselves. While genetics plays a role in gender differences, many outer forces in society deeply affect couples' mentality and behaviour in their relationships too, which then widen gender differences rapidly and imprudently. In fact, the fast-rising couples' conflicts and quarrels could be mostly attributed to the effects of social disorder, because genetics could have not changed this fast only over a few decades. Learning about gender quirks can somewhat alleviate the pressure on relationships.

Relationship Needs, Framework, and Models
L&R Series # 5
Guidelines for Success

ISBN: 978-0-9938006-9-6   **Pages:** 206   **Words:** 54,000   © 2016

The chaos in relationships nowadays disables partners to relate in a meaningful way. Instead, they seem mostly engaged in some kind of a game, or they behave passively around each other to make the best of such a frustrating entrapment.

A major source of this chaos in relationships is that couples perceive and define their 'relationship needs' as an extension of their personal needs. Some people are even more selfish and insist that their personal needs must supersede their partners' needs and any kind of *relationship needs* that might exist. They try to dominate their partners and set crooked guidelines for their relationships. In fact, we all naively assume that relationships' main (and often 'only') purpose is to make us happy.

An Excerpt

We stand at the junction of history helpless and perplexed. We do not know how to relate to one another emotionally, effectively, and efficiently. Thus, we agonize in our substandard relationships, while our personal idiosyncrasies are also mounting fast along with the rise of social complexities. Yet we are unaware of, or ignore, the hazards of our present mentality. We do not appreciate how badly the lack of relationship principles has ruined all aspects of social order. Family relationships, in particular, suffer nowadays both in terms of child rearing and couples' ability to communicate, as human interactions keep becoming less sincere and manageable. Instead, partners' over-sensitivity and dogmatism are shortening relationships' longevity. Overall, the stress level in society has been rising daily because we ignore the current cultural deficiencies—especially the absence of Generally Acceptable Relationship Principles (GARP) to guide couples.

Works in Progress

The title of this booklet hints about many other books, at least another dozen, that I am working on presently and hoping to release gradually during the next decade if my life, stamina, and writing habits let me complete the pending projects. There will be sequels for two of the published novels, *Persian Moons* and *Midnight Gate-opener*. A new novel is also underway. However, most of my efforts are devoted to the completion of 8-9 nonfictions in the areas of relationships and social life.

The new books would continue to emphasize on the same theme and objective noted on pages 5 and 7. We must know and acknowledge our mental, lifestyle, and social weaknesses in order to improve them.

Acknowledgments

I must thank only my muse for helping me write and edit these books extensively, or maybe only fooling me to keep writing. She even forced me to set aside my passion for painting seven years ago to focus only on writing, although many people and experts believed my painting were quite good. She even woke me up often in the middle of the nights to write down her good suggestions. A few other people whose judgments I trusted partially, including my son, did not find time or interest to read these books and give me a reliable feedback. Yet I would like to thank them, too, for making me laugh and boost my spirit.

Ordering the Books

Printed books are available at:
Amazon.com, Amazon.ca
Contact@Erosbook.net
Some independent bookstores in Canada
eBook versions:
www.amazon.com/Kindle-eBooks
www.Kobobooks.com

www.ingramcontent.com/pod-product-compliance
Lightning Source LLC
Chambersburg PA
CBHW060706280326
41933CB00012B/2325